THIS NOTEBOOK BELONGS TO :

_____

CONTACT NUMBER/EMAIL :

_____

THIS BOOK WAS MADE BY:

PHOENIX CREATIONS

Thank you for your support!

Order Date		Order #

>>> · <<

Customer Name		

Contact Number		

Email		

Delivery Address		

Delivery ☐ Pick Up ☐	Delivery or pick up date	

Order Details	Quantity	Flavors

Customer Specific Requests

Payment Method

Online ☐
Cash ☐
Credit ☐

Notes

Total Amount Charged: $

Design Request

Order Date   Order

❧>>·<<❧

Customer Name

Contact Number

Email

Delivery Address

Delivery ☐	Delivery or pick up date	
Pick Up ☐		
Order Details	Quantity	Flavors

Customer Specific Requests

Payment Method

Online ☐
Cash ☐
Credit ☐

Notes

Total Amount Charged: $

Design Request

Order Date

Order

❧❥❥ • ❦❦❧

Customer Name

Contact Number

Email

Delivery Address

Delivery ☐ Pick Up ☐	Delivery or pick up date	
Order Details	Quantity	Flavors

Customer Specific Requests

Payment Method

Online ☐
Cash ☐
Credit ☐

Notes

Total Amount Charged: $

Design Request

Order Date | Order

>>> • <<<

Customer Name

Contact Number

Email

Delivery Address

Delivery ☐	Delivery or pick up date
Pick Up ☐	

Order Details	Quantity	Flavors

Customer Specific Requests

Payment Method

Online ☐
Cash ☐
Credit ☐

Notes

Total Amount Charged: $

Design Request

Order Date   Order #

⤳>> • <<⤳

Customer Name

Contact Number

Email

Delivery Address

Delivery ☐ Pick Up ☐	Delivery or pick up date	
Order Details	Quantity	Flavors

Customer Specific Requests

Payment Method

Online ☐
Cash ☐
Credit ☐

Notes

Total Amount Charged: $

Design Request

Order Date	Order #

>>·<<

Customer Name

Contact Number

Email

Delivery Address

Delivery ☐ Pick Up ☐	Delivery or pick up date

Order Details	Quantity	Flavors

Customer Specific Requests

Payment Method

Online ☐
Cash ☐
Credit ☐

Notes

Total Amount Charged: $

Design Request

Order Date	Order #

>>·<<

Customer Name

Contact Number

Email

Delivery Address

Delivery ☐ Pick Up ☐	Delivery or pick up date

Order Details	Quantity	Flavors

Customer Specific Requests

Payment Method

Online ☐
Cash ☐
Credit ☐

Notes

Total Amount Charged: $

Design Request

Order Date   Order #

>>> · <<<

Customer Name

Contact Number

Email

Delivery Address

Delivery ☐ Pick Up ☐	Delivery or pick up date	
Order Details	Quantity	Flavors

Customer Specific Requests

Payment Method

Online ☐
Cash ☐
Credit ☐

Notes

Total Amount Charged: $

Design Request

Order Date	Order #

>>> • <<<

Customer Name

Contact Number

Email

Delivery Address

Delivery ☐ Pick Up ☐	Delivery or pick up date

Order Details	Quantity	Flavors

Customer Specific Requests

Payment Method

Online ☐
Cash ☐
Credit ☐

Notes

Total Amount Charged: $

Design Request

Order Date   Order

⊰❯❯ • ❮❮⊱

Customer Name

Contact Number

Email

Delivery Address

Delivery ☐	Delivery or pick up date	
Pick Up ☐		
Order Details	Quantity	Flavors

Customer Specific Requests

Payment Method

Online ☐
Cash ☐
Credit ☐

Notes

Total Amount Charged: $

Design Request

Order Date   Order

➤➤ • ◄◄

Customer Name

Contact Number

Email

Delivery Address

Delivery ☐ Pick Up ☐	Delivery or pick up date

Order Details	Quantity	Flavors

Customer Specific Requests

Payment Method

Online ☐
Cash ☐
Credit ☐

Notes

Total Amount Charged: $

Design Request

Order Date	Order #

Customer Name

Contact Number

Email

Delivery Address

Delivery ☐	Delivery or pick up date
Pick Up ☐	

Order Details	Quantity	Flavors

Customer Specific Requests

Payment Method

Online ☐
Cash ☐
Credit ☐

Notes

Total Amount Charged: $

Design Request

Order Date　　　　Order

>>> · <<<

Customer Name

Contact Number

Email

Delivery Address

| Delivery ☐ | Delivery or pick up date |
| Pick Up ☐ | |

Order Details	Quantity	Flavors

Customer Specific Requests

Payment Method

Online ☐
Cash ☐
Credit ☐

Notes

Total Amount Charged: $

Design Request

Order Date	Order #

>>> · <<<

Customer Name

Contact Number

Email

Delivery Address

Delivery ☐	Delivery or pick up date
Pick Up ☐	

Order Details	Quantity	Flavors

Customer Specific Requests

Payment Method

Online ☐
Cash ☐
Credit ☐

Notes

Total Amount Charged: $

Design Request

Order Date   Order

≫≫ • ≪≪

Customer Name

Contact Number

Email

Delivery Address

Delivery ☐	Delivery or pick up date	
Pick Up ☐		
Order Details	Quantity	Flavors

Customer Specific Requests

Payment Method

Online ☐
Cash ☐
Credit ☐

Notes

Total Amount Charged: $

Design Request

Order Date   Order

>>> • <<<

Customer Name

Contact Number

Email

Delivery Address

Delivery ☐	Delivery or pick up date	
Pick Up ☐		
Order Details	Quantity	Flavors

Customer Specific Requests

Payment Method

Online ☐
Cash ☐
Credit ☐

Notes

Total Amount Charged: $

Design Request

Order Date   Order

⤛⤜ · ⤛⤜

Customer Name

Contact Number

Email

Delivery Address

Delivery ☐ Pick Up ☐	Delivery or pick up date

Order Details	Quantity	Flavors

Customer Specific Requests

Payment Method

Online ☐
Cash ☐
Credit ☐

Notes

Total Amount Charged: $

Design Request

Order Date

Order

Customer Name

Contact Number

Email

Delivery Address

Delivery ☐ Pick Up ☐	Delivery or pick up date	
Order Details	Quantity	Flavors

Customer Specific Requests

Payment Method

Online ☐
Cash ☐
Credit ☐

Notes

Total Amount Charged: $

Design Request

Order Date		Order #

>>>·<<<

Customer Name

Contact Number

Email

Delivery Address

Delivery ☐ Pick Up ☐	Delivery or pick up date	

Order Details	Quantity	Flavors

Customer Specific Requests

Payment Method

Online ☐
Cash ☐
Credit ☐

Notes

Total Amount Charged: $

Design Request

Order Date

Order

❦≫ · ≪❦

Customer Name

Contact Number

Email

Delivery Address

Delivery ☐	Delivery or pick up date	
Pick Up ☐		
Order Details	Quantity	Flavors

Customer Specific Requests

Payment Method

Online ☐
Cash ☐
Credit ☐

Notes

Total Amount Charged: $

Design Request

Order Date   Order

❧≫ · ≪❧

Customer Name

Contact Number

Email

Delivery Address

| Delivery ☐ | Delivery or pick up date | |
| Pick Up ☐ | | |

Order Details	Quantity	Flavors

Customer Specific Requests

Payment Method

Online ☐
Cash ☐
Credit ☐

Notes

Total Amount Charged: $

Design Request

Order Date	Order #

>>> · <<<

Customer Name

Contact Number

Email

Delivery Address

Delivery ☐ Pick Up ☐	Delivery or pick up date	
Order Details	Quantity	Flavors

Customer Specific Requests

Payment Method

Online ☐
Cash ☐
Credit ☐

Notes

Total Amount Charged: $

Design Request

Order Date   Order #

&>>> · <<<&

Customer Name

Contact Number

Email

Delivery Address

| Delivery ☐ | Delivery or pick up date |
| Pick Up ☐ | |

Order Details	Quantity	Flavors

Customer Specific Requests

Payment Method

Online ☐
Cash ☐
Credit ☐

Notes

Total Amount Charged: $

Design Request

Order Date   Order

Customer Name

Contact Number

Email

Delivery Address

| Delivery ☐ | Delivery or pick up date |
| Pick Up ☐ | |

Order Details	Quantity	Flavors

Customer Specific Requests

Payment Method

Online ☐
Cash ☐
Credit ☐

Notes

Total Amount Charged: $

Design Request

Order Date

Order

>>> · <<<

Customer Name

Contact Number

Email

Delivery Address

Delivery ☐	Delivery or pick up date	
Pick Up ☐		
Order Details	Quantity	Flavors

Customer Specific Requests

Payment Method

Online ☐
Cash ☐
Credit ☐

Notes

Total Amount Charged: $

Design Request

Order Date   Order

>>·<<

Customer Name

Contact Number

Email

Delivery Address

Delivery ☐	Delivery or pick up date	
Pick Up ☐		
Order Details	Quantity	Flavors

Customer Specific Requests

Payment Method

Online ☐
Cash ☐
Credit ☐

Notes

Total Amount Charged: $

Design Request

Order Date	Order #

>>•<<

Customer Name

Contact Number

Email

Delivery Address

Delivery ☐ Pick Up ☐	Delivery or pick up date	
Order Details	Quantity	Flavors

Customer Specific Requests

Payment Method

Online ☐
Cash ☐
Credit ☐

Notes

Total Amount Charged: $

Design Request

Order Date		Order #

>>> · <<<

Customer Name

Contact Number

Email

Delivery Address

Delivery ☐ Pick Up ☐	Delivery or pick up date	
Order Details	**Quantity**	**Flavors**

Customer Specific Requests

Payment Method

Online ☐
Cash ☐
Credit ☐

Notes

Total Amount Charged: $

Design Request

Order Date	Order #

> > · <<

Customer Name

Contact Number

Email

Delivery Address

Delivery ☐ Pick Up ☐	Delivery or pick up date

Order Details	Quantity	Flavors

Customer Specific Requests

Payment Method

Online ☐
Cash ☐
Credit ☐

Notes

Total Amount Charged: $

Design Request

Order Date	Order #

>>·<<

Customer Name

Contact Number

Email

Delivery Address

Delivery ☐ Pick Up ☐	Delivery or pick up date	
Order Details	Quantity	Flavors

Customer Specific Requests

Payment Method

Online ☐
Cash ☐
Credit ☐

Notes

Total Amount Charged: $

Design Request

Order Date	Order #

>>> · <<<

Customer Name

Contact Number

Email

Delivery Address

Delivery ☐	Delivery or pick up date
Pick Up ☐	

Order Details	Quantity	Flavors

Customer Specific Requests

Payment Method

Online ☐
Cash ☐
Credit ☐

Notes

Total Amount Charged: $

Design Request

Order Date	Order #

>>> • <<<

Customer Name

Contact Number

Email

Delivery Address

Delivery ☐	Delivery or pick up date
Pick Up ☐	

Order Details	Quantity	Flavors

Customer Specific Requests

Payment Method

Online ☐
Cash ☐
Credit ☐

Notes

Total Amount Charged: $

Design Request

Order Date	Order #

Customer Name

Contact Number

Email

Delivery Address

Delivery ☐	Delivery or pick up date
Pick Up ☐	

Order Details	Quantity	Flavors

Customer Specific Requests

Payment Method

Online ☐
Cash ☐
Credit ☐

Notes

Total Amount Charged: $

Design Request

Order Date	Order #

⊱⟩⟩ · ⟨⟨⊰

Customer Name

Contact Number

Email

Delivery Address

Delivery ☐ Pick Up ☐	Delivery or pick up date

Order Details	Quantity	Flavors

Customer Specific Requests

Payment Method

Online ☐
Cash ☐
Credit ☐

Notes

Total Amount Charged: $

Design Request

Order Date	Order #

>>·<<

Customer Name

Contact Number

Email

Delivery Address

Delivery ☐ Pick Up ☐	Delivery or pick up date	
Order Details	Quantity	Flavors

Customer Specific Requests

Payment Method

Online ☐
Cash ☐
Credit ☐

Notes

Total Amount Charged: $

Design Request

Order Date	Order #

>>·<<

Customer Name

Contact Number

Email

Delivery Address

Delivery ☐ Pick Up ☐	Delivery or pick up date

Order Details	Quantity	Flavors

Customer Specific Requests

Payment Method

Online ☐
Cash ☐
Credit ☐

Notes

Total Amount Charged: $

Design Request

Order Date	Order #

>>> · <<<

Customer Name

Contact Number

Email

Delivery Address

Delivery ☐	Delivery or pick up date
Pick Up ☐	

Order Details	Quantity	Flavors

Customer Specific Requests

Payment Method

Online ☐
Cash ☐
Credit ☐

Notes

Total Amount Charged: $

Design Request

Order Date	Order #

>>➤ ‣ ⫷⫷

Customer Name

Contact Number

Email

Delivery Address

Delivery ☐ Pick Up ☐	Delivery or pick up date	
Order Details	Quantity	Flavors

Customer Specific Requests

Payment Method

Online ☐
Cash ☐
Credit ☐

Notes

Total Amount Charged: $

Design Request

Order Date	Order #

>>·<<

Customer Name

Contact Number

Email

Delivery Address

Delivery ☐ Pick Up ☐	Delivery or pick up date

Order Details	Quantity	Flavors

Customer Specific Requests

Payment Method

Online ☐
Cash ☐
Credit ☐

Notes

Total Amount Charged: $

Design Request

Order Date	Order #

>>> • <<<

Customer Name

Contact Number

Email

Delivery Address

Delivery ☐ Pick Up ☐	Delivery or pick up date	
Order Details	Quantity	Flavors

Customer Specific Requests

Payment Method

Online ☐
Cash ☐
Credit ☐

Notes

Total Amount Charged: $

Design Request

Order Date	Order #

>>> · <<<

Customer Name

Contact Number

Email

Delivery Address

Delivery ☐ Pick Up ☐	Delivery or pick up date	
Order Details	Quantity	Flavors

Customer Specific Requests

Payment Method

Online ☐
Cash ☐
Credit ☐

Notes

Total Amount Charged: $

Design Request

Order Date   Order

⟫ ⟩⟩ · ⟨⟨ ⟨

Customer Name

Contact Number

Email

Delivery Address

Delivery ☐	Delivery or pick up date	
Pick Up ☐		
Order Details	Quantity	Flavors

Customer Specific Requests

Payment Method

Online ☐
Cash ☐
Credit ☐

Notes

Total Amount Charged: $

Design Request

Order Date	Order #

❧⤜ ⟫ • ⟪ ⤛❧

Customer Name

Contact Number

Email

Delivery Address

Delivery ☐ Pick Up ☐	Delivery or pick up date

Order Details	Quantity	Flavors

Customer Specific Requests

Payment Method

Online ☐
Cash ☐
Credit ☐

Notes

Total Amount Charged: $

Design Request

Order Date	Order #

>>> · <<<

Customer Name

Contact Number

Email

Delivery Address

Delivery ☐ Pick Up ☐	Delivery or pick up date

Order Details	Quantity	Flavors

Customer Specific Requests

Payment Method

Online ☐
Cash ☐
Credit ☐

Notes

Total Amount Charged: $

Design Request

Order Date	Order #

>>‧<<

Customer Name

Contact Number

Email

Delivery Address

Delivery ☐ Pick Up ☐	Delivery or pick up date	
Order Details	Quantity	Flavors

Customer Specific Requests

Payment Method

Online ☐
Cash ☐
Credit ☐

Notes

Total Amount Charged: $

Design Request

Order Date	Order #

❱❱ • ❰❰

Customer Name

Contact Number

Email

Delivery Address

Delivery ☐ Pick Up ☐	Delivery or pick up date

Order Details	Quantity	Flavors

Customer Specific Requests

Payment Method

Online ☐
Cash ☐
Credit ☐

Notes

Total Amount Charged: $

Design Request

Order Date	Order #

⤜➤➤ • ⟨⟨⤛

Customer Name

Contact Number

Email

Delivery Address

Delivery ☐ Pick Up ☐	Delivery or pick up date	
Order Details	Quantity	Flavors

Customer Specific Requests

Payment Method

Online ☐
Cash ☐
Credit ☐

Notes

Total Amount Charged: $

Design Request

Order Date	Order #

>>> • <<<

Customer Name

Contact Number

Email

Delivery Address

Delivery ☐	Delivery or pick up date
Pick Up ☐	

Order Details	Quantity	Flavors

Customer Specific Requests

Payment Method

Online ☐
Cash ☐
Credit ☐

Notes

Total Amount Charged: $

Design Request

Order Date   Order

>>> • <<<

Customer Name

Contact Number

Email

Delivery Address

Delivery ☐ Pick Up ☐	Delivery or pick up date	
Order Details	Quantity	Flavors

Customer Specific Requests

Payment Method

Online ☐
Cash ☐
Credit ☐

Notes

Total Amount Charged: $

Design Request

Order Date	Order #

❧❯❯ • ❮❮❧

Customer Name

Contact Number

Email

Delivery Address

Delivery ☐ Pick Up ☐	Delivery or pick up date

Order Details	Quantity	Flavors

Customer Specific Requests

Payment Method

Online ☐
Cash ☐
Credit ☐

Notes

Total Amount Charged: $

Design Request

Order Date	Order #

─>}}・{{<─

Customer Name

Contact Number

Email

Delivery Address

Delivery ☐ Pick Up ☐	Delivery or pick up date

Order Details	Quantity	Flavors

Customer Specific Requests

Payment Method

Online ☐
Cash ☐
Credit ☐

Notes

Total Amount Charged: $

Design Request

Order Date   Order

Customer Name

Contact Number

Email

Delivery Address

Delivery ☐ Pick Up ☐	Delivery or pick up date	
Order Details	Quantity	Flavors

Customer Specific Requests

Payment Method

Online ☐
Cash ☐
Credit ☐

Notes

Total Amount Charged: $

Design Request

Order Date	Order #

>>·<<

Customer Name

Contact Number

Email

Delivery Address

| Delivery ☐ | Delivery or pick up date |
| Pick Up ☐ | |

Order Details	Quantity	Flavors

Customer Specific Requests

Payment Method

Online ☐
Cash ☐
Credit ☐

Notes

Total Amount Charged: $

Design Request

Order Date	Order #

>>> · <<<

Customer Name

Contact Number

Email

Delivery Address

Delivery ☐	Delivery or pick up date
Pick Up ☐	

Order Details	Quantity	Flavors

Customer Specific Requests

Payment Method

Online ☐
Cash ☐
Credit ☐

Notes

Total Amount Charged: $

Design Request

Order Date   Order

❧≫ · ≪❧

Customer Name

Contact Number

Email

Delivery Address

Delivery ☐	Delivery or pick up date	
Pick Up ☐		
Order Details	Quantity	Flavors

Customer Specific Requests

Payment Method

Online ☐
Cash ☐
Credit ☐

Notes

Total Amount Charged: $

Design Request

Order Date	Order #

>>> • <<<

Customer Name

Contact Number

Email

Delivery Address

Delivery ☐ Pick Up ☐	Delivery or pick up date

Order Details	Quantity	Flavors

Customer Specific Requests

Payment Method

Online ☐
Cash ☐
Credit ☐

Notes

Total Amount Charged: $

Design Request

Order Date	Order #

Customer Name

Contact Number

Email

Delivery Address

Delivery ☐	Delivery or pick up date
Pick Up ☐	

Order Details	Quantity	Flavors

Customer Specific Requests

Payment Method

Online ☐
Cash ☐
Credit ☐

Notes

Total Amount Charged: $

Design Request

Order Date	Order #

❧>> · <<☙

Customer Name

Contact Number

Email

Delivery Address

Delivery ☐ Pick Up ☐	Delivery or pick up date	
Order Details	Quantity	Flavors

Customer Specific Requests

Payment Method	Notes
Online ☐ Cash ☐ Credit ☐	

Total Amount Charged: $

Design Request

Order Date	Order #

>>•<<

Customer Name

Contact Number

Email

Delivery Address

Delivery ☐ Pick Up ☐	Delivery or pick up date

Order Details	Quantity	Flavors

Customer Specific Requests

Payment Method

Online ☐
Cash ☐
Credit ☐

Notes

Total Amount Charged: $

Design Request

Order Date	Order #

⊱⪢ • ⪡⪡⊰

Customer Name

Contact Number

Email

Delivery Address

Delivery ☐ Pick Up ☐	Delivery or pick up date

Order Details	Quantity	Flavors

Customer Specific Requests

Payment Method

Online ☐
Cash ☐
Credit ☐

Notes

Total Amount Charged: $

Design Request

Made in the USA
Monee, IL
19 April 2021